I0012010

Disclaimer:

While the author hopes that this book will be valuable and helpful for you or your business, they cannot make any guarantee that the steps within are appropriate for your situation, or guarantee increase in profits or any other improvements as a result of implementing steps or ideas from within this book.

All information is accurate at the time of writing, and to the authors knowledge, however no liability will be accepted for any inaccuracies that may accidentally occur.

You carry out or implement any advice within this book entirely at your own risk.

Advice and steps within this book should not be seen as a substitute for seeking legal or professional advice or help.

Introduction

During the COVID-19 pandemic in 2020 I created a new product –
PittRecipes – following the increased interest in baking. Over a
month, I planned and released the first version.

(You can download PittRecipes for free from my website at
www.libraryplayer.co.uk)

While creating PittRecipes I wrote a series of blog posts on creating
PittRecipes and software products in general, and after writing
several posts I decided to turn it into this book!

Within these pages you will find some of the original blog posts,
relevant posts I've written previously and updated, plus plenty of
new content too.

Whether you are interested in creating and releasing a software
product yourself, any other type of product within your small
business, or just interested in how something is put together and
released, then I hope this book has something for you.

This is not another book on how to write code – in fact there are
barely any coding and very little code examples – these are my own
experiences with creating, planning and releasing PittRecipes and
my other products.

It's not a bunch of theory, made up stuff or academic teachings either – this book is based on my own experiences, and what is REALLY involved with creating new products.

For a developer – writing code can be the easy part. However there are many other aspects too – deciding how the application is going to work and planning on paper, testing, marketing (which itself needs to be planned) and so much more.

A lot of the principles and ideas in these books don't just apply to software either – they can apply to many other different types of products, or aspects of running a small business too!

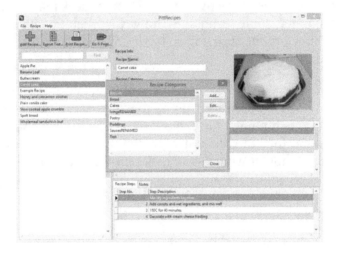

Before you write a line of code

Putting the idea to paper!

Many people believe that when someone comes up with an idea for a software product, they immediately go to their computers and write code.

Often that is not the case however - yes some ideas may be tried out on the computer, some techniques, however when I come up with an idea for a new product I first need to sit down with a pencil and paper, and plan!

- How is the application going to store data? Which database tables is it going to use, types of data, etc. Decisions will be mode - for example in my recipe book application I needed to decide how it would store different weight measurements!

- Which development tools am I going to use? Which database technologies?

- How is the application going to look? Who is going to use the application? How will the different screens appear?

- How will everything work? Often even the simpler tasks are a bit more complex and require a bit more thought with a pen and paper!

- Desktop application (and even then - Windows, Linux, Mac or even all of them?)? Mobile app? Web-based system? A mixture of all of these?

- What will the application actually do? What is the minimum required to get a first version out there, and hopefully get some feedback?

- Are there any new technologies, tools or techniques you'll need to learn?

- Testing the logic that you've already put to paper (yes its not just code that needs to be tested)!

- Actually designing the different components of each part of the application.

All this will save a significant amount of time when it actually comes to writing your code.

Plus there is the business side to things...

- Market research - will anyone actually use the application? What will they want or expect? As a side note I'll add that it's good to get a basic version out there, even if it doesn't include everything.

- Are you going to release a beta version to get feedback, or just release a basic first version? I have my own thoughts on this - perhaps I'll write a separate post on this.

- Planning out time to create the application.

- Budgeting - are there any additional development tools or third party components you'll need to purchase? More staff required?

- Legal - making sure you protect the copyright to your software.

- Help from others - whether that is additional staff/team members or a business partner to help sell your new idea.

- Deciding on pricing.

- Additional services that can be offered - for example help transferring data across.

- Planning how the application will be marketed and promoted.

Not all of these will be worked out right away - however it's good to have at least some initial thoughts. Software is much more then code - and all of this will need to be planned!

And all this before I've even written a line of code!

How do I come up with product ideas?

It's a question I sometimes get asked - and the answer is it can depend for each product.

Sometimes I'll come across charities that are still using paper or spreadsheets for their membership details (and even having multiple versions of membership records!), or sometimes I'll need a to-do list software, can't find anything suitable, and will therefore develop one myself, and release it as a commercial product.

One of my audio applications was developed because I saw something a charity was using, and thought I could create something better, which then get turned into a useable product.

With my application launcher that I released in 2019 - PittLaunch - I came up with the idea after discussions at networking events and online with people that where fed up with Windows 8 and Windows 10, particularly with the way applications are launched.

There are plenty of Start menu replacements, or utilities that can return features from earlier Windows versions to Windows 8/10 - however I decided to create a product with the following goals:

- It wouldn't take over a computer, or make any major changes to the system.

- Could be used alongside any existing software/setup.

- Avoid adding unnecessary features, and focus on stability - e.g. skins may look great, however they can be distracting and get in your way.

- And create something different (and easier to use) then other similar applications.

The end result was PittLaunch - which occupies a window in the screen. You can add shortcuts to your favourite applications so you can quickly access them - and even split them into different categories (also handy when you have LOTS of icons on your desktop). There's also easy access to your Start menu items at the top of the window, plus a menu with links to items on your desktop, plus common system functions.

I also tried something different with PittLaunch - and created a version that can be trialled without installing - and have since starting looking at ways at making this possible with my other applications.

My most recent product is PittRecipes (notice a pattern with the names?) - which I developed while writing this book.

During the COVID-19 lockdown in 2020, there was an increased interest in home baking – with supermarkets even struggling to stock flour.

As someone who has had an interest in home baking – even before the lockdown – that is how I came up with the idea for PittRecipes. Just over a month later – with a lot of planning and development (much of which is covered within this book) I released the first version.

What do version numbers actually mean?

If you look at my website (**www.libraryplayer.co.uk**) you'll notice that many of my products use years instead of numbers for version numbers. This is something I started doing a few years ago.

The advantages of this include...

- Years mean more to users then a number – for example they can see that the 2018 or 2019 release is the most recent version. Version 4.3 for example may not mean as much.

- Its particularly useful when providing product support and asking what version is currently in use.

- For internal use I still use a version number as well.

There are some disadvantages...

- If there is more than one release a year, e.g. bug fixes, etc. I usually get around this by changing the version number rather than the year, appending a letter to the end of the year (e.g. 2019a) or indicating there is an update (e.g. "2019 update 1").

- Using a traditional version number can help demonstrate how established and mature a product is – for example version 4 or version 4.1.

- For a product that has just launched (for example PittLaunch which was released earlier in the year – www.pittlaunch.co.uk) a version number does not really matter.

- Using years for products that are not updated as regularly may give the appearance that something is out of date (e.g. if you are looking at version 2014 of a product, and its 2019) – I'd note however this is far from the case – and sometimes older products can work just as well (if not better) then newer versions – think how long Windows XP and Windows 7 have been in use.

What do version numbers actually mean?

- These can vary depending on company and developer – however this is my system (which is sometimes flexible).

- A product version with a single number (e.g. version 2 or version 2.0) indicates a significant new version since the previous release – for example major changes, lots of additional new features or new technology being used.

- A product with a decimal number (e.g. version 2.1) indicates a minor release – there may be a few new features, existing features may be improved, however there are not lots of changes.

- Can go even further – for example if I make one or two minor changes or fix bugs, and the product remains mostly the same as the previous version, I'll attach an additional number or a letter at the end of the version number (e.g. version 2.1.1 or version 2.1a).

Version numbering from other developers can often be interesting and sometimes just marketing – for example Windows 7 is actually Windows 6.1. And there is not even a version 10. Other developers sometimes skip version numbers so they can match the version numbers of their competitors (e.g. if a company has version 3 of their product, and a competitor has version 6, they'll release the next version of their own product as version 6 to match).

Breaking larger tasks down into smaller tasks

When creating a new product, there are often some big scary looking tasks.

The easy way to deal with these is to break them down into smaller tasks. The result will be that the task will seem less scary, and help you focus on each individual part.

Here's an example (it's not a software development example – it's one I used from one of my planning blog posts, however the principle is very much the same) - imagine you have the following task within your list:

Add a calendar booking system.

This can seem daunting - and you may even try to put it off until the last minute. Instead think about what you need to do for this task, and break it down into smaller tasks:

Decide on a day and time for the meeting.

Find a venue for the meeting.

Book the venue for the meeting.

Create an EventBrite or booking page.

Contact group members to let them know about the meeting.

Process bookings and follow-up any enquiries.

Set up meeting venue on the day.

There could be more that you could add to the list - it does illustrate my example well.

While a fairly long list, it does make the task less scary. Focus on one part of the task at a time - and do that really well - for example booking the venue. Thinking about completing a sub-task is easier then thinking about the whole thing!

Can also make it easier to delegate, if you have a team that you can delegate to! For example, you could ask another member of your team to book the venue, while you create the EventBrite page.

When creating a software product, its also important to not avoid putting those big tasks off – get them done. Many of the smaller tasks and features often depend on those big tasks – sometimes in ways you don't expect (e.g. when validating data).

Depending on what needs to be done, create a separate test application for that big task, before incorporating it into your new product. Again, this helps you focus on the big task (especially when you follow the example above) and makes testing much easier too.

No cutting edge features here!

As someone who creates and develops software products - the title of this post may sound like an odd thing for me to say - surely I should include the latest cutting edge features, technologies, ideas and techniques in my products?

Let me begin by asking you a question - **how many software products or websites that have the latest clever features have you used, that ended up crashing, being unreliable, frustrating or causing all sorts of problems?**

Be honest - would you prefer something that works, works really well and is easy to use without any hassle?

And that is the philosophy I adopt with my products.

I try to include everything that users need within their products - however I avoid anything unnecessary or that could cause instability.

The other thing I do is to try and stay faithful to how the operating system intends things to be, where possible. For example, I don't see the need to draw my own scrollbars or toolbars when Windows provides a perfectly good one!

(And yes, there are a lot of products that manually try to draw their own items, or have their own titlebars rather than using the Windows ones, which consumes extra memory).

Does this mean my products are behind the times? Absolutely not!

Or that they are not as easy to use? Actually - because I don't include the flashy stuff that gets in the way, they are often much easier to use!

Most of the "cutting edge" features and things people need are most often still there - without the bells and whistles and flashy screens.

Very few features may be missing - however these are things that are hardly used, if at all.

Would you prefer to drive a car that had the latest gadget and needs to go in for repair every week, or prefer a proven make and model, that does the job really well and hardly needs any maintenance?

What NOT to put in your application!

I recently had a bit of a sort out on my computer. Disabling items that where automatically starting up, and changing settings in software that was not performing as expected. Quite astonishing really - and a lot of things I'd never include or put in my own products!

(Side note: it's worth checking your own computer and software settings, disabling items that shouldn't really be automatically starting up, and reviewing settings in your web browser and other things you use regularly)

So here are things I would NEVER put in any of my products (and if you develop software I hope you don't fall into the trap of doing the same again)...

- Automatically sending usage information to the developer. Yes I found a lot of applications doing this, without even checking with me - and these are well-known and widely used ones too!). If you really need or want to do this - get permission from the user first - don't just assume it's OK to do this.

- Does your application really need to load stuff up when Windows starts, and run things in the background? And I mean really? If you answered yes - are you sure? It can just end up slowing down the computer.

- Do users really appreciate the popups that suddenly appear when using Windows advertising your products, even if that product is not running at moment? See above about things running in background?

- Let the operating system do its job. For example you don't need to draw your own fancy titlebar that looks different to other Windows ones - this consumes more memory and can slow your application (and anything else that may be running).

- Yes installing updates can be important - especially with your operating system and antivirus tools - however what control do you give your user over updates? Do they have the option to check for and/or install updates manually?

- No - I don't want to also install Google Toolbar or anything else while installing or updating your product! If I want to use Google Toolbar, I'll go and get it myself.

- An easy to use application that looks great is excellent - however remember the easy to use part and don't make it difficult for users to use your software.

- Don't break a previous version of a product if someone is happy with the current version and chooses not to upgrade or buy the latest release.

- No scare stories or false information to try and sell your stuff! For example, I saw an "expert" try and scare people into buying and signing up with their product, because it "would be against GDPR" if they didn't - and it was clearly not the case.

- Have a web based application? Make it easy for users to actually sign out (it's astonishing how many websites hide them nowadays - lots of people still check their things at work or on public computers you know)!

- And don't automatically assume that people want you to remember their login details either. Yes it's nice to have that option - and that is exactly what it should be - an option.

- Finally - another web-based one - no people don't want to like your Facebook page, they don't want to sign up for your newsletter, they don't want to... you get the idea, all those popups on your website just get in the way - people want to read the information, and if they like you then there is a time and a place for everything else!

A lot of the above may seem clever - however they are not. And they slow down people's computers. And cause all sorts of problems.

Is there anything you can add to the above list? For example things you've come across in software products, or

Create a good or excellent product - and create it really well!

Which programming language?

There are so many (possibly a lot more than many realise) programming languages out there - some much more popular than others.

C#. Java. Delphi/ObjectPascal. C++. Swift. SmallTalk. Fortran. COBOL. Visual Basic. Pearl. Python. And so many others.

Some languages are designed for specific purposes (e.g. maths, data, etc.), others are interpreted or scripting languages. And many others are general purpose.

And many companies have their own compilers and tools for a particular language.

So when creating a new software product, which language are you going to use? And which development tools?

It can be tempting to go with the most popular one.

Or go with one designed for your specific area of business.

However my answer is a simple (and somewhat controversial one) - use whichever language you are happy with, and is best for your product or business.

Want to use Visual Basic? Go ahead!

Or Delphi? Again - go ahead!

I can hear some people saying - **"what if that language is outdated?"** - I hear this a lot with products made in less widely used languages, or ones that where popular years ago and don't receive much attention these days.

However if you have a closer look, you'll find those "outdated" languages are more popular then you think - and still widely used - and will continue to be for many years and decades to come.

So don't just pick something because it seems like the modern one or most popular - pick the right tool for the job!

Desktop, cloud or mobile apps?

"Everybody is using the cloud now!"

"Your product must be web based!"

These are two things I've heard a number of times - the idea that desktop software is now obsolete. However they are statements and ideas I disagree with.

OpenOffice. GIMP. Audacity. And many more - they all have one thing in common - they are desktop based applications.

There are many advantages to desktop software too - you don't need subscriptions, rely on a service that could close down, and the software can make use of the user's system resources.

Also worth considering that not everyone has reliable Internet access.

Am I saying that web apps are a bad thing? And that software shouldn't be cloud based? No I'm not - I am saying that both desktop and web based applications have a place, market, demand and advantages.

And then there are mobile apps. Although it's not an area I've gone into yet.

When coming up with an idea for an application - decide which type of application will be best for your product - and more importantly the people using them.

If you wanted - you could even have a mixture (a desktop version, mobile version and an online version).

Don't just make it web based because that seems to be the trendy thing at the moment!

Coding & Implementation

Trying new ideas and tools!

When creating a new product, it can often be essential to use a new set of tools, parts of existing tools you've never used before (even with something you may have used for 20 years!), third party components or techniques.

It can be tempting to just get them, set them up and then use them to create (or with) your new software product immediately.

Not a good idea!

Take some time to learn new tools you have obtained for your project. And I don't mean spending 10 minutes reading the quick start guide or watching a YouTube video! Spend some time experimenting with the tool, properly learning it. Even if that takes an entire day - or even a week!

It's worth it - not just for your current project, with future projects too.

Create small test applications for any new techniques you need to try.

And of course test the test applications. Really test them. Try to destroy them - try to break them - try to cause them to crash - to ensure that you have the required validation and checks to ensure they don't!

Read the documentation if you need to - and I mean really read it (even if it does look a bit scary!)

For example, if you have never created a database using code before (or using a different tool to do so), spend some time with some smaller test applications to try this out - rather than creating the database for your product right away.

Here's one I recently created - I'd decided to use another tool for a new idea to create a database - rather than diving straight in I created a few test applications. This one testing connecting to and creating a database.

While I'd done the same many times in other tools before - and doing so here was almost identical, there was still some quirks and minor differences. I was glad I tried the idea out first, before creating the main piece of software.

All this also applies to anything you may not have used for a while.

And if something is not working - then it's good to identify that now then halfway through your project - was that really the right tool, project or component? Are there alternatives you can look into?

You'll often do this with each separate part of your application as well - develop each part individually (e.g. the database creation code, code for downloading things from the web, etc.) so that they can be tested individually and thoroughly before being integrated into the main application.

Don't always need new ideas!

While creating my recipe book application, I've talked a lot on experimenting on new ideas and techniques (some of which could make their way into my other existing products if they go well) - however it's also amazing how many existing ideas and components are going into the new product.

Over the years, there is a lot of code I've written that can be (and often is) reused in my other applications - need code for writing database information to settings? Already got that! Code for accessing particular folders, or data in a database? Or code to display an "About" window for the application? Got them too!

I don't have to write everything from scratch - there is a lot of stuff from previous projects that go into new ones. I've often written them in a way that are modular and therefore can be easily reused.

Some of this code has existed. Why rewrite it? Why reinvent it? Imagine - all those years of bug fixes! All those years of tweaking and improvements to get them working well.

(Side note: if anyone ever suggests rewriting a software product from scratch, the above same arguments can be used for not doing so - and there are a lot of great blog posts and articles out there that advise against this for the very same reasons)

And imagine the time its saving me too - rather than writing them from scratch I can just drop them into my new product, significantly speeding up development time.

And it's not just my code either - there is a lot of great third party components that can (if their license agreement allows!) to be used within my products, saving more time.

Doesn't just apply to code either - there are templates for documentation, templates for license agreements.

Looking at it another way as well - I've mentioned there are new ideas I'm trying in my products - imagine how those will be improved over the years, as they are incorporated into new products, and future ones I've not even thought of yet.

You could also argue there is an element of skills that apply here too - in addition to existing components, there are the skills that I (and many developers) have learned and picked up over the years.

Much of this doesn't just apply to my own products - it could apply to products from other software developers too. In fact, it could apply to many types of products - publications that use templates, new workshops that use previous methods for teaching, etc.

So for all the talk of innovation, there is a lot (and possibly a lot more than many realise) of existing ideas, tools, components and techniques in new software products.

Errors only developers can make!

Let's briefly take a break from all the serious stuff within this book, with this chapter.

I've just written a function. Got it working perfectly. And then I run my application - click the button to test it - and it didn't work - what happened?! Don't worry - its at that point that I realised I forgot to actually get the code to run when the button is clicked!

And that has inspired this section - just for fun here is a list of mistakes and errors I've made while developing new products...

- There is the one I've already mentioned - writing code and then forgetting to associate it with a menu or button, causing much confusion.
- Writing documentation, clicking within my application wondering why nothing is happening, and then realising I'm clicking a screenshot!
- Looking at a piece of code - wondering who wrote it - and then realising it was me many years ago.
- Using and testing the current released version of the product, rather than the development one.
- Even the most minor spelling or typing error can cause all sorts of bugs!
- Creating code to carry out a particular task - and then realising that my development tools already contain a function for that very purpose.
- Writing a new query for a database, and then forgetting to connect to the actual database.
- When working in a room with multiple computers, starting typing on the wrong keyboard and mouse!
- Not one I've had yet, and not quite an error I've made myself, however it's my list so I'll include it anyway: Spotting people

using other's products that say "prototype" or "testing version" in the titlebar - they are using a pre-release version!

- Using a similarly or identical named function in another file, rather than the one I actually intended to use.

- Temporarily renaming or removing an item, and then forgetting to change it back.

- Looking at a folder, looking for a particular file, and then realising its a folder for a different project.

I'm betting these have happened to everyone at one point or another - and if not, then there is still time!

Are there any you can add to the above list?

Or if you are not a software developer - anything similar to the above happened in your work or business?

Creating good code

When writing code for a new product (or for updating an existing one!) it's important not to cut corners, no matter how tempting it is.

It could cause problems in the long run - both for yourself - and others who may need to look at your code in the future. Or even users of the software who encounter unexpected bugs as a result - and worse because you cut corners they are much more difficult to fix too.

I've always followed the view that good code should be so well written, that even someone with no software development or computer skills could look at that code, and figure out what was going on.

This means including names for items that make sense (rather than calling things a single letter, e.g. x, which some developers choose to do) and not trying to be clever and cramming everything into one line of code (e.g. if you want to display the total of two numbers, carry out the calculation first, and then display the result, rather than carrying out the calculation on the same line of code the result is being displayed).

It really does make a difference - not just in the long term, but in the short term as well. Yes it means more work, but when you think about it - how easier it makes bugs to fixes, etc. it does make things a lot easier.

In code it's possible to include comments too - for you to describe what is going on. When I was a student at college and university, I had a reputation for including LOTS (and I mean LOTS) of comments in my code.

If the code is well written, it shouldn't really need that many comments. For tasks that may be a little more complex, for functions or particular blocks of code, it can be useful to include comments describing what is going on.

And then there is the structure of your code - important thing here is to be consistent - whether you follow your own standards or one set be an employer, client or general good practice. As long as you are consistent and the code is readable (although if it comes to choosing between the two - I always go for ensuring the code is readable, even if it means breaking the standard and structure that is set).

Don't try to be clever!

An alternative title for this post would be: **Just because you can do something, does not necessarily mean you should!**

Sometimes, it can be a minor thing, sometimes a big thing. However, sometimes it's tempting to try and be clever.

Take this line of code as an example (it's not specific to any language, and is just to illustrate my point)...

display "The total is: " number1 + number2

The above displays the total of numerical values stored in number1 and number2 - so if number1 had a value of 5, and number2 the value of 7, the following would be displayed on the screen:

The total is: 12

Looks perfectly good, right? And there is absolutely nothing wrong with the above code - and I've done this myself too.

However, I believe it's much better in the long run to get the total, and then display them, even if it means more lines of code - for example:

TotalAmount = number1 + number2
display "The total is " TotalAmount

Does exactly the same thing as the previous example, except its split into two lines of code - it calculates the total first, and then displays it, rather than trying to do it all in one go.

Which one is more readable? And easier to understand in the long run?

Now imagine the above examples being applied to an actual software product, or a large project. For example, you may wish to use the total again at a future point in time, extra validation may be required - I'm sure you could add extra examples.

And it doesn't just apply to coding - we have all used software that has unnecessary features, tries to do things in a flashy way (that end up getting in the way and becoming bloated) or don't really need to do things in a particular way and try to be clever.

It's more important that something can do the job well, without any fuss, hassle or messing around - trying to be clever or having unnecessary features can often be an obstacle and get in the way of achieving this.

And don't think it just applies to software - it can apply to a range of other situations - whether within your business or your personal life.

When you hold a workshop for example - do you really need attendees to build origami animals? Does it really have anything to do with the rest of your workshop?

A registration form or e-mail address - is it too long and add unnecessary detail (yes I'm aware there may also be GDPR issues with this!)?

Or a blog post (or section of a book) that ends up becoming really long, when you have got the point and just want to get to the end? ;-)

Difficult database fields!

While sketching out ideas for my PittRecipes software, and working out the fields that would be used by the underlying database, I came across a challenge:

How do I store details of weight measurements?

There are different units - grams, ounces, litres, cups - the list goes on!

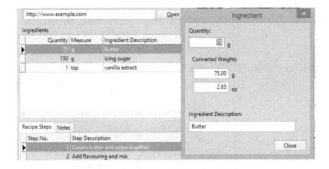

Sometimes when you come up with an idea for a new database application - many fields and columns within a database are actually a bit more complex, and require a bit more thought.

And not just in a recipe database either.

There was a few possibilities for my particular scenario:

1. Have a separate table for the different units of weight measurements - including the name of the measurement (e.g. "grams"), the shortened version that usually appears besides each measurement amount (e.g. "g") and whether it's a liquid measurement.

2. An additional text field in my ingredients table, where users could type in weight measurements each time.

3. Require users to enter a particular unit of weight measurement - which may require them to convert recipes themselves, or for the software to carry out some sort of conversion (e.g. "it uses grams, and just grams").

I ended up going with option number 1 - which meant that the application could carry out conversions to different units (with there being a gram conversion rate field in the table) while keeping the original recipe the user enters intact.

Also made the most sense when it comes to validation.

And while there may be a cleverer option out there - I didn't want to make it too complex for the user to actually enter their ingredients - don't want to scare them away from the product.

I believe the option I chose therefore has the right balance. Time will tell if its correct, or if I eventually come up with a solution I wish I'd thought of at the time!

When designing databases, chances are you will come up with similar scenarios at least a few times - I have with some of my previous products. The important thing is to sit down with a pencil and paper and give it some serious consideration - even go away and do other stuff and see if you come up with an idea (as long as you don't keep putting it off).

Sometimes there won't be a neat solution - and sometimes it may not look good on paper but will turn out a lot smarter and intuitive when you actually implement it. And of course, if your users don't like the option you chose - they will soon tell you (even if it's with their wallets and not buying the product)!

Storing images in a database

My new recipe software is the first of my products to have the option to display an image - in this case users can include a photo of the completed recipe.

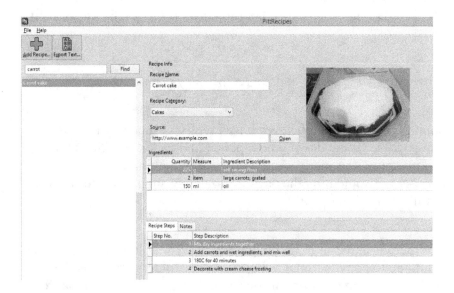

When I looked into possibilities for the best way to store a picture in the database - I found it to a topic widely debated online. Here are the two main options I considered...

1. **Store the picture itself in the underlying database.** The picture is within the database so don't have to worry about image files being moved, deleted, etc. however could lead to the database becoming quite large.

2. **Store the file path of the image, and then load the image from file.** As the path is a simple text field, takes up significantly less space in the database, however there is an issue of images not being displayed if the pictures are moved, renamed or deleted.

I went with the second option - I decided this would make the underlying database more stable and reliable, and not become bloated with too many pictures being stored within them.

When the user selects or opens a new recipe in the application, the software loads a picture (if it exists) from the location in the image file. Validation is also carried out to check if the image file actually exists.

When the user adds (or edits) a recipe, they can select the image file.

Sounds complicated, however it isn't really - especially (as with all things) after sitting down with a pencil and paper, thinking about it and planning it properly. And while it's something I will document, it's also not something the user has to worry about - as the software is still doing all the work!

Yes there is an issue if the image gets moved or deleted (one option would be to copy the image file to another folder for use by the application - however on this occasion I've not gone down that route) however I decided the benefits outweigh the disadvantages.

And the more I thought about it - I realised it's the same approach I've taken with my other applications, in a way. For example, playlists in my audio software don't contain tracks (they merely contain the location of where those tracks can be found).

Why separate data input screens?

If you have used any of my software products - or from other developers - rather than being able to edit stuff directly in search results, you have to go to a separate screen, where you can add (or in some cases) edit the data.

Here's an example from my music database software - rather than being able to add/edit details in the main screen, users of the software instead do this from a separate window:

Why set it up this way?

Why not just edit data directly into the search results or the main data being displayed?

There are various reasons why I in particular do it this way - this includes...

- Makes validation much more easier - you can ensure users have entered a particular set of data correctly before adding an item to the database.

- Some database components don't like adding data where there is more than one table in the underlying table. Even if I got it working on my computer - I could not guarantee it would work on your computer.

- Sometimes additional information may be required, that is not displayed in the main screen.

- Prevents data from accidentally being deleted, amended, etc. You don't want to carry out a simple search for something, then discover you have ruined your database (and all the effort it's taken to get it set up).

- Something that may look good in search results may not look good and be more difficult when inputting data. For example, it may be more easier to input data for a single record in a form rather than having a grid to type in.

- It may just be impossible to edit data in the search results.

- For master/detail data (where you have tables with different relationships, e.g. one record in one table has many details in another detail) entering everything in search results may be difficult and awkward.

- Allows access control to be set up for a database - particularly within a company, where you may not wish for employees to make changes for example.

- May be easier to provide a stable product rather than trying to show off with editing data everywhere.

- I've tried to set it up where data can be added/edited directly from the main screen (however it often gets messy - especially with more complicated data).

May not be a method everyone agrees with, or would use in their own products. However it's the way I continue to use (although I'm always experimenting with different methods and ways of doing things).

Myths around software products

Myths and things people will say!

It happens with most (if not all) business owners, sole traders and self employed people. Helpful friends, family and people who are suddenly "experts".

Here are some of the myths people have said when it comes to running a software business, creating and selling a product:

- **Lower your prices to get more sales** - there are so many articles out there that explain exactly WHY lowering your prices won't get you more sales, and why it's really a bad idea! Don't undervalue yourself, especially for short term gains or because others have said lowering your prices will get you more sales (and you'll end up with less in the long run anyway).

- **Nobody needs product support, so you can lower the prices or offer it for free.** Guess who the first people to ask for help and support will be (yes - the people that made that very statement!)

- **Everybody is on the cloud** - while there is more and more web software out there, there is still a demand for desktop applications.

- **It's not making any money - give up!** While I do believe you should be realistic - look at whether other factors are an issue – e.g. marketing, whether you are targeting the correct people, etc.

- **Nobody will want to use the product.** I once was told I shouldn't bother with my Member Manager software, because there are not many charities! Clearly that person never looked at the charity register - and that is just in the UK!

- **It's too niche.** Actually being too niche can be a good thing!

- **We're friends - can I have a free copy?** This is entirely up to you - however as I mentioned earlier - don't undervalue yourself or be afraid to charge.

- **Can I have a free copy in return for exposure?** And the many other variations of this too - my response is no! Just no! No! No! No! No! No! Did I say no enough times?

Are there any you can add to the list? What "helpful" advice have you been offered in the past?

What do developers know about hardware?

A myth I often come across is that because I primarily develop software - I know nothing about hardware.

Clearly not the case. And software developers do need to know about hardware.

How much memory is an application consuming? How does a sound card work so my audio application can use it? And graphics? I could go on!

And most software developers with degrees, etc. will have at least some basic training and qualifications with hardware, fixing computers, etc.

Yes, I can take a computer apart. Yes I can build or rebuild a computer. Yes I can upgrade things. Yes I can set up a basic computer network.

Indeed - I would say it's important for anyone wanting a career developing software to also gain a basic understanding of how computers work in general - including hardware.

There may be more specialist things I may not do, or be comfortable with - for example soldering. Or setting up a more complex server system and network.

(Side note: while my current business is primarily software - I have previously run a computer repair business, worked as an IT Technician and provided technical support - which yes included hardware - for a local charity)

Imagine a chef in a restaurant - they may have a particular speciality - however they still have the basic training and can cook other things as well.

The "software costs nothing to reproduce" myth!

A while ago I saw the question asked online: **Does anyone sell digital products?** Their definition was **products that have no cost to reproduce more.** This is a definition I disagree with.

While I'm talking about software here, a lot of this can apply to other digital products - for example ebooks, videos, artwork, etc.

So why do I believe that the idea that "software costs nothing to reproduce" is a myth?

- **Software will always require product support.** This includes the cost of people to provide support, make sure issues are logged, etc.

- **Customer service.** While it's rare for software to be sold in a box these days, there is still customer service to provide, questions to ask to potential customers, contacting people trialling software to find out how they are getting on, etc.

- **Marketing the products, letting people know it exists.** Takes a lot of time, effort and money.

- **Protecting the product - including copyright and ensuring data is backed up.** From ensuring there is sufficient backups in case of a disaster, to ensuring that all intellectual property is protected.

- **Server capacity.** Whether this is hosting for an online product, some files are saved online or even hosting the product for download. And not forgetting the online communities/help forums for products.

- **Documentation.** Whether its online, a PDF or a printed manual, documentation is very important, and there is the cost of writing that documentation, keeping it updated and making it available.

- **General capacity.** Does the developer have enough people within their team to provide support, or will they have to limit the amount of people that can use the software? Will they need to take on more members of staff?

- **There's also the cost for the customer.** The time it takes to download and install the product, learn how to use it, set it up to work exactly how they want to, purchasing any extras, etc.

There are many more things that can be added to the above list!

At the end of the day - even for digital products - even though they are not physical products you can hold in your hands, there is always still a cost to reproduce them.

Software is more than just code!

I've previously written about how the idea that software (and digital products in general) "cost nothing to reproduce" is a myth - and in this post I'd like to bust another myth that is somewhat similar - that software is "just code".

Some of the items in this post will be similar to the earlier post that I mention - and some will be different.

Is software really just code and a bunch of files? No its not – and here is why that is just a myth...

- Software - and even new versions of products - take a lot of planning, designing and preparation.

- Product support need to be trained on using the software - and likewise they may be expected to train, teach and help customers to use the products.

- On a similar note - companies often provide technical support and help to customers - and those that say "I don't need product support" are often the first people to end up requesting help!

- Software will be maintained - with bug fixes, improvements and upgrades.

- There will often be services around the software - for example help transferring data across, onsite training or selling equipment with software preinstalled.

- Documentation needs to be written for the software. Not just help files and manuals - also internal documentation for other developers and team members.

- Software requires a great amount of skill and effort to create. Take a cake as an example - you may have the flour, eggs, sugar and butter - however you still need someone with the know-how to actually make the cake!

- You can't just write code and then expect it to work on everyone's computers. Installation scripts and setup packages need to be created to put the software, plus all the associated documentation, etc. together so users can set them up on their computers.

- Blog posts, YouTube videos, webinars and much more may be created and available to customers to help them use the products.

- Server capacity is required - either for hosting downloads or online applications.

- There is also sometimes the costs of placing the software on, and making them available, on physical media (e.g. CD-ROM or USB disk) - although this may not be as common these days there are many products still distributed in this way.

- There is a lot of testing - this includes making sure it works on different systems, that any errors or unexpected actions are checked and don't cause the application to crash, and many more.

- On a similar note - even the preparation, designs and plans will need testing before even a line of code is written.

- Many products have years of trial and error - lots of bug fixes, plus ideas that work and ideas that don't work. Even products like Windows and Facebook took years to become what they are today.

- Many of the items in this list apply to freeware products and open source projects too - there is still support costs for the company that create them, documentation, web hosting and online communities to manage.

- Products require an entire sales process, lots of marketing, looking after customers and much more.

- Software (and many other products) are intellectual property that someone owns, spent the time creating and is copyrighted.

- While software is not a physical product that you can hold in your hands - it's still a product - that makes a difference to your life, work or business - whether its saving you time, money or making your life (and certain tasks) much easier.

Is a book just a bunch of words on paper? Or is bread from a bakery just flour, yeast and water? Is a piece of artwork just a bunch of ink, colours and paper?

You may say "yes" however I hope many of you would also say "no" to those questions - and the same applies to software too, for the same reasons.

Feature requests - more than "just a few lines of code"!

Don't let the title of this post fool you - this can apply to a lot more then software - and in many different types of products and businesses. Have you ever received a suggestion or a request for a particular feature, and been told, "it's really easy, won't take you long to do"?

With a software business - not just with my own products, but others too (including those from larger companies) I sometimes hear users and people ask, "why can't you add this feature? It will only take a few lines of code?"

(I'd note that the people saying this have probably not written a line of code for years since they were at school, if ever!)

Have you ever had requests like this or along those lines? Here's some of the reasons why adding a feature is more than "adding a few lines of code"...

- More often than not, it's much more than a "few lines of code" - for example it may require changes to an underlying database, existing data to be converted to a new format, error checking and much more.

- Even a minor feature could create much more server capacity, storage space or other requirements. For example - it could end up storing twice or three times more data.

- Product support and other staff would need to be trained on the changes.

- Documentation needs to be updated.

- Even just a few lines of code need to be thoroughly tested - do they work? Does it break any other features within the software?

- New features that are similar, identical or go in a completely different direction may already be in progress - however things take time!

- The feature request may not meet the creator's original vision for their product or business.

- The new feature may not be as in demand as people believe - even a vocal minority can be quite loud when it comes to feature requests.

- Its often better to focus on a stable product rather than features that could break things.

Am I discouraging you from considering feature requests you receive? Or contacting other companies with feature requests? Or from suggesting ideas for products you use? No - absolutely not!

Although certainly don't say that it will just be "a few lines of code" - and don't feel obliged to include or go ahead with the idea within your product.

Are there any examples you can add to the above list?

Have you ever received similar "feature requests" or ideas?

You don't always need to upgrade!

This section not only applies to you, your business or development (e.g. upgrading software development tools) – the same principles apply for your users too – sometimes they are happy using a particular version of your product, and don't want to upgrade to the latest release.

Often, I see people asking for help with an older version of a product - and there will always be at least one reply from someone trying to be clever, and saying that person should update to the latest version!

This may sound like a strange thing for someone who sells software products to say - **you don't always need to upgrade to the latest version of something!**

In fact, until recently the US nuclear weapons where still running on floppy disks! This may sound strange and alarming at first until you think about it - the software and systems they have work - they are stable - they have been tried and tested over years and decades! Why replace it with something that could potentially cause problems?

There are some developers that still use Visual Basic 6 for their development! Their code works well, and is tried and tested over years, the software they create still runs (even on newer versions of Windows) and why risk everything and break things just to follow the latest trends?

I also recently watched a documentary with a supermarket chain still using software running on Windows XP. Why not upgrade? Because the software they have works on Windows XP - again it's been tried and tested, does the job, and does the job well, so why upgrade? In fact installing the software on a newer version of Windows could cause the software to not function properly, or not produce the correct results.

Here are some more things to consider when it comes to considering upgrading...

- As already mentioned, the software and current systems work, they are stable and do the job well. Why upgrade and risk changing that? Just to use the latest big thing?

- Software development tools are another good example - code that works in one version may not work as well in future versions. Imagine all those complicated calculations, years of code, etc. that could potentially need rewritten!

- Everyone is happy using the version they currently have. And that's OK. Older versions of Windows may have issues when connecting to the Internet, however if that computer is never online, why update?

- Associated software and products may also need upgrading. Imagine the time, costs, amount of staff needed, retraining, etc.

- Older products may not work on newer systems, for example, and these products are still required.

- Rewriting could take years - plus even more time after that to fix any issues. By which point the new system will need to be upgraded to something even newer - and so it continues!

Obviously, if you need to upgrade, then that is the time to update - possibly gradually. However if a system works, and works really well, then never update just to follow a trend!

Why software won't solve all your problems!

I sometimes come across organisations or people who believe that once they purchase a particular piece of software, or get a new website set up, that all their problems will instantly be solved and go away.

However, this is not often the case:

- Getting new software can only be the start of the journey, rather than the end.

- If you have a new website, you still need to tell people you exist!

- Having software or a website does not mean you can stop marketing, recruitment, comply with any laws, etc.

- Then there is moving your existing data across to a new system!

- Yes, software can be a great help, make a big difference, save time and prove to be valuable - however you still need to put the work and effort in.

I think everyone has come across someone at some point – whether it's with software or other types of products or services, who believed that a product would solve everything.

For example, one of my products is Member Manager - which helps clubs, charities and voluntary groups manage their membership details, comply with GDPR and provides an alternative to using paper records or spreadsheets.

I'll be honest - while Member Manager can make a big difference to your organisation, as I've already indicated, it won't solve all your problems or be a "magic wand" - you still need to recruit members (although the software can help with that, e.g. monitoring how members heard about you), ensuring you are aware of what is required as part of GDPR (while Member Manager will help, you still need to be aware of what is required) and address any other challenges you are currently facing.

This is true whether you use Member Manager, PittRecipes or any of my other products, or indeed products or services from anyone else.

Assume nothing!

When creating a new software product (or any other type of product) it's really easy to make a lot of assumptions. Whether it's the way people do things, the technology they use or anything else. **However, it's important to assume nothing!**

For example - while it seems like everybody has Facebook and the latest smartphone, that is simply not the case. There are even households that don't have Internet access.

Here are some excellent examples...

- Error checking! If you ask the user to type in a number - have you made checks that they don't enter a letter? What happens if they try to type in the number as a word? Or a fraction when you expected a full number? Just because it seems obvious to type in a particular item or use something in a particular way - don't assume your users will and check for any unexpected uses of the product.

- Just because you have a high speed computer doesn't mean everyone else also has the latest model. Can users use your software on older systems?

- On a similar note - just because something runs on your computer doesn't mean it will run on everyone else's.

- Not everyone has Internet access. Yes, really!

- Many people choose not to have a Facebook profile or any other form of social media. Again - yes, really!

- And not everybody has a smartphone either.

- Have you made it as easy as possible for people to contact you with any questions or requests for assistance? For example - with both online and offline methods?

- Your software may not be for everybody - have you made it as easy as possible for people to remove it from their computers?

- Remember that not everybody has the same IT skills as you - and may struggle with using a computer and need more help.

- Is there anything you can do to make your software easier to use for people with disabilities?

Are there any examples you can add to the above list? Either in relation to creating a software product, or any other type of item or product?

And it's impossible to account for every possible scenario and situation - for example your Windows software may not run on Apple Macs, may require newer or particular pieces of hardware, etc. And it can also depend on who your product is targeting.

However - the original point remains - never assume anything about the people (or computers) that will be using your software product.

Millions of users overnight is a myth!

Have you ever watched those Hollywood movies, where someone creates a new app, and then the next morning they have millions (or billions) of users and are rich, etc.? And it's a myth people often have in the real world too!

However, its simply not the case (although if it does happen for you, I will be delighted).

The reality is that creating and releasing a new product takes a lot of time, effort and patience, and sometimes even years to establish themselves.

Look at Facebook, Apple, Microsoft and many others - although it doesn't feel like it, it took them years to become the companies they are today. With many ups and downs.

Anyone remember (or actually used) Windows 1 or 2? Or did you have a Facebook profile when it first launched (which is unlikely since it started as a website for use by students at the same university as Mark Zuckerberg and grew from there)?

The reality is for many software products you won't have people instantly downloading your product within a few hours or 24 hours.

For a start, it takes a lot of marketing - don't even think of adopting the "build it and they will simply come" mentality. Just not going to happen. People need to know you exist - and that is not just with a website. It's with continuing to engage with your potential users, getting listed in online directories, contacting potential clients and so much more!

Many software products take a while to become established. That is the same with products from big corporations, and my own products.

My Member Manager software took a few versions before it really lifted of and people started talking about it. The same with my to-do list software.

There is also a lot of refinement and improvement. Getting a first basic version out there - and improving it over time - including based on feedback, improving existing features, fixing bugs and adding features you didn't have time to add in the initial release.

You have a small customer base to begin with? That's a good thing - focus on building that small loyal following - make sure you keep that user base loyal, and grow your product from there.

Ignore those that say that just because a few people - or barely anyone - is using your product that it is a flop. It isn't. As I've helpfully helped illustrate.

(I will add a small note here to still be realistic and identify what is not working, if the product is targeted at the right people, if there really is any interest, etc.)

And don't just develop the product, release it and expect stuff to happen. Go out there and promote your product. Talk to those using it, trying it and those it could help. And most importantly - be patient!

Help, Support & Documentation

Documentation for users!

When creating a software product - there is the documentation you write for yourself and for your project internally (and there are many books, blog posts, etc. out there dedicated to that topic) and then there is documentation to help your users.

As a minimum there is a help file.

Sometimes there will be a manual too - remember in the 80s and 90s buying software in big boxes and receiving thick heavy manuals? These are often PDFs nowadays. And often the content is the same as the help file (including in my products - where the help file is converted from the user guide).

However - what do you include in your help file and manual? Basic steps with how to use each feature of the software. Perhaps practical examples as well? Or how to carry out a solution to a particular problem or use of the software?

And there is potential for all sorts of documentation and help for your users online - for example blog posts (related to your industry and how your product can solve them), YouTube videos, news, tips, and much more.

Plus you may have a "readme" file with information the user should know before and after installing - often displayed as part of the installation itself.

And then there is the license agreement? Have you ever read one (so much interesting things in there when you look)? License agreements are something you should consider seriously, whether they are basic terms you set out yourself, use a template, or you want to get something professionally written. Some of the things in my license agreement may sound obvious - for example "this product can not be used for any illegal activities" - plus the usual disclaimers and warranties.

There's hints and tips you could display when the application starts (which I've recently introduced in some of my products).

And of course, you can go down the late 90's Microsoft Office route and introduce a talking paperclip - although I've resisted temptation to introduce this in my products myself!

The important thing - your documentation is easy to read and follow by users of your products (yes, even the license agreement - especially with GDPR, etc. where terms and conditions, privacy, etc. need to be easy to follow and understand)!

And the documentation needs to be easy to access as well - whether that is clicking a help button, visiting your website or even typing in your product name from Google.

(Side note: manuals and documentation often provide an insight not just to users of your products, but potential users as well, who are considering your product and check out the documentation to see what its really like - so do bare this mind)

No jargon - no technical details if you can avoid it - users want to know how to do something within your product - no messing around!

Helping and supporting users

In addition to creating and releasing software - I also have to take into consideration how I'm going to provide product support to anyone using the software.

This includes making it easier for people to contact me from within the software itself (something I've worked on improving over the past few years), making it easier for anyone to contact me from my website, etc.

Whether you are a one-person business, or have a whole team or can outsource, being able to provide product support is a must!

- **Don't just provide "copy and paste" answers.** These are frustrating, especially when they don't even answer the question someone asked.

- **"I won't need product support"** - this is an argument I sometimes hear from people wanting my products at a lower price. Never accept this point. And I can bet money on who the first people to contact you for support will be (yes you guessed correctly, the people that said that statement)!

- **"Can you do this for me?"** - while answering any enquiries is a must - you will need to decide how to include more detailed help. For example - you may provide basic support and answer questions at no additional cost, and then charge extra for more detailed support, e.g. installing the product for them, transferring data across or on-site training.

- **Set a time limit for basic support.** Especially if your software is not available on a subscription basis, and you are happy for people to continue using the software after the support period ends.

- **What happens when your application crashes?** There will always be a problem on someone's computer - when something goes wrong how easy to you make it for customers to contact you?

- **Options to fill out a survey at the start of a trial period or when installing are good things - secretly collecting data is not!** Don't be tempted to gather usage data - your users really won't appreciate it. The option to fill out a survey is a good thing though.

- **Product available to people for free?** Consider how you will provide product support in this situation - are you happy to answer any questions free of charge? Will users have to pay for or purchase at least basic support from you? Or perhaps set up a forum or Facebook group where users can ask questions, help each other and reduce answering duplicate enquiries (since you only need to answer questions once, and everyone will benefit from the answer). This is something I'm currently considering with my recipe software.

When deciding on the pricing of your product - take into consideration the product support you will provide. Advertise this along with your products too - e.g. "includes 12 months product support and updates".

Either way - being able to, and ready to support those who use your products is a must, and not something to include as an afterthought.

No copy and paste answers please!

Have you ever contacted a company's product support department - possibly sent them an e-mail, and then received an answer that was clearly copied and pasted? Either from a standard set of answers, or from someone else's response?

A few times I've contacted product support for a piece of software I use (and it's from a large, widely known business too), and I've received such answers - it's almost as if they didn't read my question! Sometimes they even refer to the wrong version of their product that I'm using - or the wrong version of Windows. Or its an answer to a completely different problem that is not related to mine. Or even a mixture of all these.

This can be frustrating - not only have they not helped me, it causes delays in fixing the issues that I have, and therefore delays in getting my work done. One time I even had to get help from a third party to resolve the problem.

Would you use a product from a company that you know would do this? Or recommend them to others?

Ever since I started my business in 2012, I've always prided myself on being honest, and I would never use copy and paste answers.

- Yes it's good to have a log, note or set of "standard" answers that you can use - however make sure that when you use them, you don't just copy and paste - tailor it for your client, and make sure it actually answers their question.

- Actually read your clients question. Understand their problem.

- If you can't help them, find someone who can. Even if that means letting them know that you plan to get back to them as soon as you can, as you need to check with other people that can answer their question more effectively.

- Make sure you are responding to the correct products and versions! Even if it's no longer supported, at least ensure you carry out any obligations to them, e.g. ensuring they have license keys to active their product on a new machine.

- If you have to outsource your product support, make sure it's of the same (or higher) standard that you would expect from your own department.

- In the long run, copy and paste answers don't reflect well on your company's reputation.

- Remember - these are paying customers that you are helping. And potential repeat customers.

And what can you do if you constantly receive copy and paste answers?

- As I've previously mentioned, get help and support from a third party. Although this can prove costly, and may be a last resort.

- Wait a few days - and try contacting at a different time/shift to see if someone else responds to your enquiry.

- If the product support department won't help - try contacting their sales department instead. Yes, they may try and sell you their latest version or model - however you are more likely to speak to someone who won't fob you off (they want you to buy stuff!) and help you with your enquiry in the process (they want to keep you as a customer and don't want you moving to a competitors product) - if they tell you to contact product support, mention the problems you have been encountering.

- Contact the company via social media (e.g. Twitter or Facebook) posting on their company's profile. The fact a different department will see your message can also help.

- Depending on your problem, look at moving to a competitor's product. Again this may be a last resort.

Additional ways to help!

One piece of advice I'd always give to someone considering selling a software product is to never rule out the additional help and support you can provide users of your products.

Sometimes it may even feel like the main part of the business, and the most profitable, with the actual product being secondary.

For example...

- **Offering to help move existing data across.** While your product may include options to make this easier, users may not wish to spend the time doing this themselves, and would prefer to pay you to do this. Or they may still be uncomfortable with attempting it themselves.

- **Installing the software on their computer or premises for them.**

- **Developing bespoke versions.** This is a topic that is debated with developers of software products - whether bespoke versions of products should be developed for people - it can often distract from the main product you sell.

- **Additional companion products**.

- **Enhanced product support beyond the basic help you supply.**

- **Access to a free Facebook group for users of your products**, or a mailing list/support forum.

You could do some of these yourself - or even work with third party suppliers or companies if you prefer - as long as it's the same high standard you'd expect. Some of the above you may offer for free, while others you may wish to charge for.

Make sure you have a proper plan in place, and that it doesn't distract you from the main product you develop.

I would add that the most important thing is to help people using your products, and help them really well, and not just rush the job to make a quick buck.

Releasing your product

Version one versus a beta release?

There are two ways of getting feedback on a new product:

1. **Release a beta version** and get feedback from the people trying the product. Perhaps rewarding with a discount on the first release to anyone trying the product.

2. **Release a basic first version** and then improve the product based on feedback. For example the first version could be free (or low cost) with plans to pay for a future release.

Of course, you could try a mixture of both.

I've tried both with varying results - and they have their own advantages and disadvantages.

I've found getting feedback on a beta release can be difficult - with having to chase people up - and if you go down this route create a survey, keep in touch with people trying.

A basic first version - released as soon as possible - which is the option I go with nowadays is great for getting initial feedback from as wide a group as possible. Again you still need to actively encourage feedback - although with social media this can be easier.

What feedback do you want from users of the products? How do you consider feature requests, and whether to implement them? How do you deal with bug reports, and more importantly fix them?

There are so many questions - and ideally try and sort them out before releasing a beta version. Put together a questionnaire - possibly using Google Forms or SurveyMonkey if you go with either option.

And of course it can depend on the nature of the product itself.

With beta versions make sure people trying the product are not just your friends and family - you want to receive honest feedback. And that it isn't just people wanting a free copy to play with.

Not an easy answer - and if you develop and release a software product something you'll need to consider and work out for yourself.

I'll end this post with one final note - there is a "Hollywood movie" style myth where many believe that you'll get hundreds and thousands of people signing up and adopting software on the first day of release. Doesn't happen. Even products like Windows and Facebook took years to become what they are today. Be patient and while you should be realistic - **keep going!**

The best day for release!

Whether it's a brand new product, or a new version of an existing product - the release needs to be planned, including deciding which day of the week it will be released on!

In the past, I've tried different days of the week for releases, with different and varying results - including Monday, Wednesday and Thursdays. In recent years, I've settled on Wednesdays as the best day of the week for release. Although I may change my mind again at some point!

Let's have a look at each day of the week...

1. **Monday** - everyone is recovering from the weekend, and catching up with e-mails, etc. from over the weekend. They have a lot to do, and don't necessarily have time to look at your new product.
2. **Tuesday** - Slowly getting back into the working habit after the weekend, however now they have caught up with their e-mails still have a bit of work to do so don't have time to look at your product.
3. **Wednesday** - halfway through the week, chances are got through their work, and slowly starting to think about the weekend and their plans for next week. A bit more relaxed now - and more likely to have a look at any new things coming their way.
4. **Thursday** - getting those deadlines and everything completed before the weekend starts.
5. **Friday** - it's almost the weekend, they want to finish work so don't want to look at your new thing, because its more stuff to do!
6. **Saturday & Sunday** - for many people they are not working, and if they are, they want to complete their work so they can have the rest of the weekend off.

You may agree or disagree with the above. And I've exaggerated and simplified it a bit - and of course every person is different - however I hope the above has helped illustrate my point and logic!

It can also depend on who your product is targeted towards.

One interesting idea I read from another developer a while ago - they release new versions of their product on Friday. That gives home/personal users a chance to download and use their product over the weekend, and to fix/resolve any issues that may arise ready for Monday when the business users start using it!

It's an excellent idea that I love - and one that I may try for myself at some point when I have a product targeted towards both home and business users.

Also remember - regardless of which day you release the product, people simply won't just come along and download it. You need to do lots of promoting, and let people know it exists and how it can help them on an ongoing basis.

Release days are a great way of generating interest in your product - so it's definitely worth planning and preparing, rather than just making it up as you go along (or just putting the files online for download) - however it shouldn't be the be all and end all - continue to promote your new release.

Apologies if I haven't given you a definite answer - consider who uses your product - experiment with different days and find out which days work well for you.

Protecting your product!

If you are releasing a commercial product - you'll need to consider how you are going to protect your product, and add copy protection.

The prospect can seem a little bit scary, and it may even take the fun out of developing and creating your product.

However it's important to consider. How can you stop people copying the software onto more machines then they are licensed? Or giving away copies to friends?

There are many third party copy protection components out there - or you may wish to create your own (e.g. locking the software license to a particular machine or requiring users to enter a serial code after they have registered/brought from you).

I'm going to be brutally honest - chances are you won't be able to completely stop it - people will always find ways and workarounds.

You also don't want to scare away potential users too much.

And if a license is locked into hardware then you may need to provide them with a new license key if they choose to move their license to a new computer.

The most important thing is to deter people.

And if you find people redistributing licenses for your software online - then don't be afraid to put a stop to it. Contact them (depending on who they are). Contact their web host. Do whatever it takes to protect your product.

If you discover personal users, business users or charities using the software on more computers then licensed, or giving license keys away, then don't be afraid to do something about it. Whether it's a formal written "remove those copies" letter, a sales letter, invoice, or phone call - or a combination of steps. It's your product - and you have a right to protect it.

(Remember that business and charity users will not want their reputations damaged by using unlicensed software - or for that fact to be made public - so you could use that to your advantage)

Doesn't just have to be copy protection within your product - for example depending on the contract you could ask for an annual audit from commercial users, send them a sales e-mail if you notice they are using the software on more computers then registered, etc.

What goes into a license agreement?

When you install most software products, you will see a license agreement of some description (whether it's an open source agreement, or a commercial agreement) - terms and conditions which you must agree to before you can install and use the software.

(Although I've seen a few applications display a license agreement when you first run the application - although a bit cheeky to get someone installing something first, and then getting them to agree to terms and conditions!)

Whether you hire someone to create an agreement (could be a lot of legal fees!), use a template or create an agreement yourself - what should go into a license agreement?

Not an easy one to answer, and can depend on the product and terms under which you want to release it. However, here are a few things to consider that I've put into mine...

- **The software must not be used for any illegal activities.** Sounds obvious, doesn't it? Does it really need to be included? I have it in there as a disclaimer to protect myself - i.e. if someone uses it for any illegal activities - whether its pirating music tracks or more serious crimes - it's against the terms and conditions, so removes some liability on my part, and makes it easier to pursue people that may use the software for such purposes and get them to stop.

- **You are responsible for complying with any data protection laws, including GDPR.** This one is particularly important with my membership software - while it can help with GDPR compliance, the person using it is ultimately responsible for compliance (and any consequences as a result of non-compliance).

- **You are responsible for the security of your data.** This is on a similar note to the previous example.

- **Liability for any damage caused, loss of data, etc. from use of the software** - while your product is thoroughly tested, include these anyway to be on the safe side.

- **Copying and redistributing the product.** Remember - it's your product, so include terms under which copies of the software and license keys can be redistributed.

- **Could your software product potentially be used to create a rival product?** Are you happy for this to happen? Not something I've had to include in my products - however something worth considering depending on the nature of your product.

- **How much product support and help will users receive from you?**

- **If you offer a trial edition, or a free lightweight edition, include terms under which these are made available.** For example, that users are not permitted to try and extend the trial, or hack the software to get a full edition license.

- **Privacy and data you may hold or collect about the user** - including GDPR, how you use the registration information users provide, etc. Although you may wish to include this as a separate notice on your website, depending on what you are doing.

- **Third party components that may be used within your product** - I include a general disclaimer in mine - e.g. the application may include third party files and components, e.g. DLL files that are required for the product to run, that are the copyright of their respective owners. I also include that I am not associated or part of the development of these components, and that users should contact me in the first instance if they require product support.

- **At the bottom of the agreement, I include contact details for if someone has any questions about the license agreement** (if someone is unsure, it's much better that they ask!) - although to date nobody has asked me about anything in the license agreement.

There are many scenarios above which many never occur or be needed, however they are in there as a safety net.

Don't feel overwhelmed by the above list and examples. Most of them are straightforward, and it won't take as long as you may initially think to put together the agreement.

Don't worry about trying to be clever or including legal jargon - in fact a license agreement that is easier to read may be preferable.

Include a license agreement of some description - even if its basic terms and conditions you have typed up yourself.

In a final side note, I will add it is worth reading license agreements for many widely used commercial applications - it's really interesting (and sometimes a little bit surprising or shocking) what they put in there.

(As a disclaimer, I will add that this section should not be considered a substitute for seeking professional or legal advice)

Installation packages!

I've created a great new software product - and now I need to get it on to the users computers as easily and as pain free as possible.

I do this by putting together an installation package.

I use a tool called Inno Setup which thankfully makes this really easy - although a bit of scripting know-how is still an advantage.

The installation package puts all the required files together - the main application executable, plus anything it needs to run - together into a single file. Plus any documentation and other components that may be included with the software.

And there are the different installation steps - displaying a readme file with basic information, the license agreement, selecting which parts to install and more.

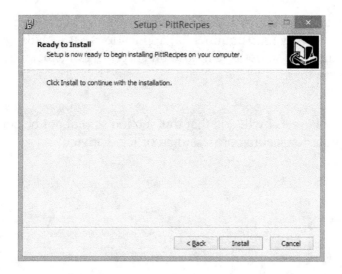

In the past year or two - I've decided that less is more - and try to include as few steps as possible. For example while displaying the license agreement is possible, does it really need to display the readme file? Do users really need to select the components or do they just want the thing on their computers?

One thing I've recently included at the end of installation is the option to fill out a short survey, so people trying my products can let me know what they expect, what their problems are and how they hope my products can help solve them. Received some great feedback so far. If you include this - make sure its optional as well.

Don't forget to make it easy for users to uninstall the software too. I've also given users the option to fill out a short survey - although unlike other products its optional and not thrown in the users face - as it's nice to get their feedback on why they may wish to remove the product, and help me improve them.

When I released my PittLaunch application launcher in 2019 - I've also experimented with creating a version that can be trialled without installing. Users may not necessarily want to install a software product they have just come across.

The important thing is that the installation should not be neglected - and should make the software as painless and as easy as possible for the user to install (and uninstall if they wish to do so) from their computer!

Promoting

Promoting your product

If you expect to be able to just put a software product online, and then expect everyone to download it, then you are mistaken!

Marketing and promoting my own products is something I have found challenging - and still continue to work on.

If you want to create and sell a software product - marketing is something you will need to learn. There are many books, blog posts and articles on the topic - and I highly recommend reading these.

Don't just look for IT or software marketing help either - read books on general marketing, particular areas of marketing, etc. Find the right books and resources for you - if something works then try something else. More importantly actually follow and try the steps in any books or articles.

If you are looking for recommendations for good books to read, you are welcome to join my book group on Facebook (members outside Aberdeen also welcome) at:
facebook.com/groups/AberdeenBusinessBooks

Also - don't just think you can post a few things on Facebook and that's your marketing done - it really isn't.

There are of course marketing courses available too.

Don't be afraid to ask for help - and I mean proper help (not the friends who are suddenly "experts" at marketing). Join some good and supportive Facebook groups. Hire a marketing agency if you can afford it and wish to do so. Take on board a business partner with a marketing background, if its someone you know and trust (although do put a formal agreement in place).

When promoting a software product, here are some ideas and things you can try...

- Submit your products to any relevant online directories or listings.

- While not as relevant today as 10 or 20 years ago - you can submit your product to download websites (e.g. Softpedia). Make sure these are reputable websites though, services that attach toolbars, etc. to your product won't do well for your reputation. You can create a PAD file however I find I get a better response submitting my products manually to a few good websites.

- It's not just online marketing - consider writing letters to potential clients, phoning people, etc. depending on who your product is targeting.

- Remember - it's not what your product does. It's how it helps people, make their life easier and solve a particular problem. Try and get potential users to imagine using your product, and get them to imagine the difference it can make for them.

- Don't give up! Be realistic - however if your product is not doing well - is marketing the reason, and something you need to improve or approach differently?

There are so many other possibilities too.

I have a spreadsheet with a template marketing plan - each time I release a new product (or a new version of an existing product) I refer to this template, adapt/tailor it where appropriate and then import into my to-do list software.

Remember marketing and promoting your product isn't just something you do when you launch or release - it's something that needs to be done on an ongoing basis.

And I apologise for referring you to other resources - however I will repeat that marketing is something you will need to get to grips with - and could cover an entire series of blog posts (or books) in itself.

Don't ask for an e-mail address!

How often do you see an offer for a free download or product... and all you have to do is provide them with your e-mail address?

Many people have said I should do the same with the free downloads and trials of my products - however it's something I've decided against!

- When you are in this situation - how often do you enter your e-mail address, and how often do you just decide it's not worth the hassle and go and find something else?

- And when you do enter your e-mail address - is it your actual e-mail address that you check all the time, or a throwaway e-mail address you set up just for situations like this? Be honest!

- Its more work for the person interested in your product - they want your free download or trial - don't create any barriers or unnecessary steps for them!

- When you do send them your fabulous newsletter or marketing e-mails, even if they do receive them, how often do they actually read them? And how often do they just click the Delete button?

- Reduces a bit of the pressure, and seems more honest. You genuinely want them to try what you offer - you are not just trying to harvest their contact details.

- I often include the fact that they don't need to register or provide an e-mail address as an advantage in my marketing. How refreshing it sounds - they get to try something for free, without the usual hassles that seem to be everywhere these days.

In recent years, after installing one of my products, users have the option (note: an option - not automatically throwing it in front of their faces) to fill out a short survey. This helps me discover what challenges they are facing, and how my products will help them.

This includes an option for them to enter their e-mail address if they are happy to contact me to discuss further - however this is an optional field (so they can send the survey without the e-mail address) - and if I do contact them, it's to find out how they are getting on with their trial, NOT to add them to any newsletters or send them lots of marketing e-mails.

Also - they don't have to fill out the survey, its displayed as an option **after installing the product** - i.e. I've not made it a condition of getting the download in the first place.

And of course, there is GDPR - however there are entire books out there on that subject!

Honesty

I believe in being honest - if I can help you, great! If I can't, hopefully I can point you in the direction of someone who can!

I never take on work that I can't actually do.

Years ago, I wrote this list on how I'm honest - and it's still the same today:

- **Never saying something is not working or needs replacing when it works perfectly fine, just to make extra money.** I will work to make sure any existing software or equipment works with your existing products.

- **Providing you with as much information as possible about any technical work carried out.**

- **No spyware, intrusive features or any other nasties in our software.**

- **Identifying the best equipment and software for your requirements, even it means recommending a competitors product!**

- **Working alongside and with any existing technical staff or contractors, and not against them.**

Sounds simple, straightforward and common sense? You could even say it sounds obvious? Because it is!

How are you honest within your business?

Beyond the Release

I've released the first version, what's next?

After almost a month of development, I released the first version of PittRecipes!

I decided to make it available free of charge (with the option to buy me a coffee) for a number of reasons - including its target market (primarily home users), the fact it's a basic first version, etc.

Between coming up with the idea, planning, and actually creating the product, PittRecipes possibly took the shortest amount of time to get out there. Mainly because I experimented with a different model (i.e. getting a basic first version out there, rather than a fully featured first version). In total, it took just under two months.

So, what's next?

- Continuing to develop and improve the product, including adding options that I have planned and didn't make it into the first version.

- Taking on board all the feedback I receive from the first version (although ultimately I will still make the final decision when it comes to priorities, what is included in future versions, etc.)

- Review the first version - what worked well? What aspects could be improved? Was there anything that could be improved with releasing and promoting the product? Already a few things I want to work on (particularly improving how new recipes are added).

- Having a few days off - particularly from writing any code or software development.

- Marketing doesn't stop when a product is released - so continue to promote the product.

- A great response to the release so far - however I will monitor the reaction to the first version over the next few weeks and months.

- I have other products so those will continue to be developed and worked on as well. Indeed PittRecipes includes some new ideas that may make their way into my other products.

Overall – continuing much of what I cover within this book – which doesn't just apply to brand new products, but existing ones too, and on an ongoing basis!

Planning the next versions

How do I plan for future versions of my software?

I often plan or two versions in advance, and keep a record of my plans using my own to-do list software, PittStop.

There are features and options that I feel need to be implemented right away - and there are others that, while still important - can wait.

Especially during the early days of a product - the first version can often be very basic, with extra new features and options you'd planned from the start being included in later versions. It's tempting to do it all in the second release, however do take your time, implementing a set of features in the next release, more in the following release, etc.

When adding a major new feature - adopt the same approach as a basic first version. Get a basic version of that new feature working, and then improve it over time. I remember doing this with the Events option in my Member Manager software - getting the basics in one of the releases in 2015, and then improving on it over the next few releases.

Sometimes I'll think of an idea, note it down, and then a day or two later, upon reflection, it's not really that great. Other times I will add it to the to-do list for the next version.

Sometimes I may feel it's more appropriate for the version after the next version.

Sometimes while I'm working on a new version of a product - I'll look at the item or task, and occasionally reconsider whether it's appropriate upon reflection - especially if it's a while since I added it to the list. Sometimes I'll move it to the next release (although if you keep doing this, it's probably not a great idea after all, and you should just cancel or delete that item).

If you are currently developing a new version of a product, don't be tempted to add your new idea into that version! Unless it's a bug fix, add it for the version after the one you are currently one.

Whether you have a to-do list database like mine, or notes on a bit of paper, do sit down and plan the next version and what you'll include. Rather than just opening your software development tools and making it up as you go along!

And finally...

Whether you plan to release a product of your own, or just wanted to learn a bit more about how a software product is created and released, I hope you enjoyed reading this book, and found some of the information valuable.

I'd love to hear your feedback – including anything you have found valuable within this book and will implement yourself.

Send me an e-mail at **simon@libraryplayer.co.uk**

I also encourage you to revisit this book – whether its re-reading particular sections, or going back and trying some of the things for yourself.

And I regularly post blog posts on LinkedIn on creating software products – among other things – it would be great to connect with you at: **linkedin.com/in/SimonPittman**

Also by the author

- **Editing Audio Using Audacity**

- **Managing a WordPress Website**

- **How to Develop Software**

All the above books are available on Amazon!

www.ingramcontent.com/pod-product-compliance
Lightning Source LLC
La Vergne TN
LVHW051536050326
832903LV00033B/4270